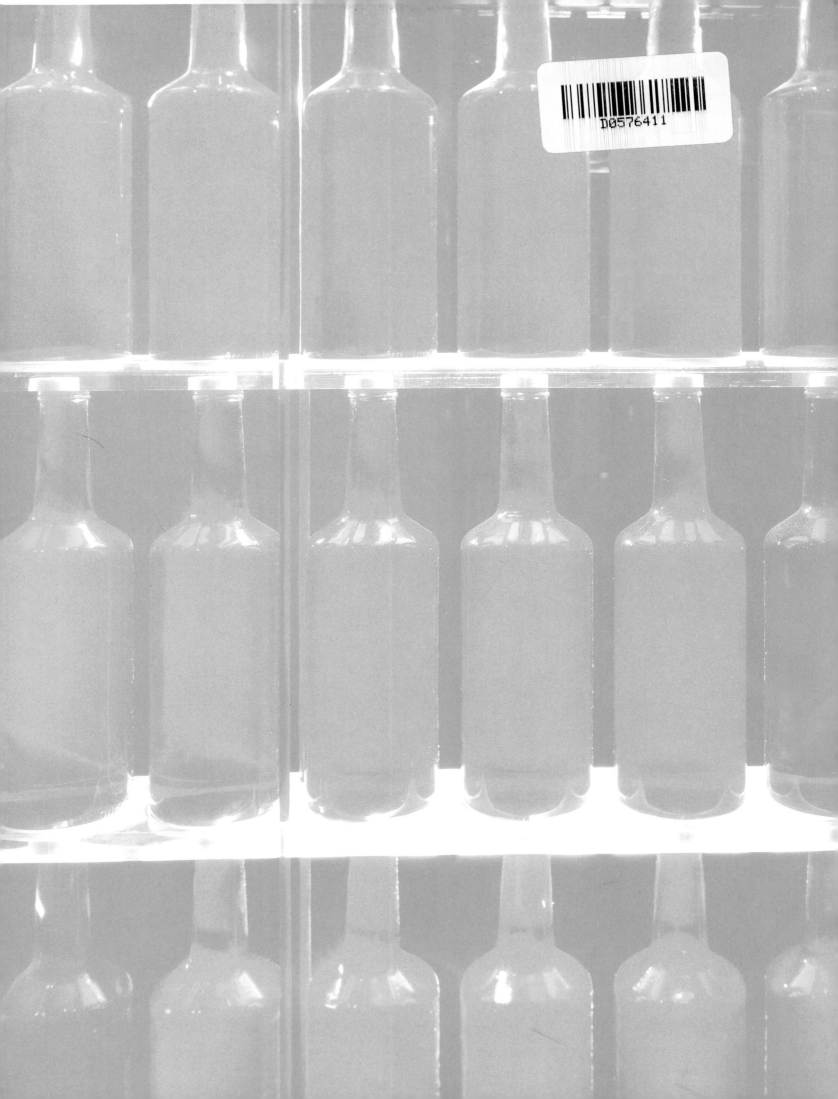

BARS

PUBS

CAFÉS

ROCKPORT

Copyright © 2000 by Rockport Publishers, Inc.

All rights reserved. No part of this book may be reproduced in any form without written permission of the copyright owners. All images in this book have been reproduced with the knowledge and prior consent of the artists concerned and no responsibility is accepted by producer, publisher, or printer for any infringement of copyright or otherwise, arising from the contents of this publication. Every effort has been made to ensure that credits accurately comply with information supplied.

First published in the United States of America by
Rockport Publishers, Inc.
33 Commercial Street
Gloucester, Massachusetts 01930-5089
Telephone: (978) 282-9590
Facsimile: (978) 283-2742
www.rockpub.com

ISBN 1-56496-653-4

10 9 8 7 6 5 4 3 2 1

Design: Leeann Leftwich, Stephen Perfetto
Cover Image: Paul Warchol

Printed in China.

BARS PUBS CAFÉS

GLOUCESTER MASSACHUSETTS

ROCKPORT PUBLISHERS

Hot Designs for Cool Spaces   Julie D. Taylor

CONTENTS

STYLE, AMBIANCE, & DESIGN

Given a set of circumstances, there is only one way to design a restaurant. The trick: you have to find it. That way can be Nature or God, or whatever you want to call it. The most precious part of the design process is when you see something—a starting point, a theme—that inspires your own creativity.

You might say, "Wouldn't it be wonderful if the whole table could light up?" You must treasure your ideas and not let others dissuade you. It may be difficult to do, but usually what's heavy, expensive, and difficult is what's good.

When I design an interior, the most important thing to me is lighting. Lighting is the focus, and everything else must serve the focus. Anything else is secondary.

Once you find your focus, you can then move from the general to the specific. Do not

FOREWORD

Michael Chow

be afraid, as William Blake once wrote, to "see the world in a grain of sand." Design bit by bit, and recognize that specific details make the whole.

Designing, to me, is like arranging a collection of fine art gathered through time. Instead of a painting, I may be collecting a bridge, a railing, a wall, an obelisk, or a hinge. They all stay in my mind's library until I need to use them.

Collecting elements, however, is not enough. You need to make them your own. You have to personalize them. The more personal, the more universal. You have to have a relationship with each object before you put it in a space. And, if everything has your stamp on it, then when you put all these materials together, they will be harmonious. If a space is harmonious, then even the air becomes great.

Art is a very important element in all my interiors and in my life. The wonderful artist Keith Haring prepared this portrait, "M. Chow as Green Prawn in a Bowl of Noodle," in 1986. Green Prawn is a specialty of the house at Mr. Chow restaurants, and was Keith's favorite dish.

Style, attitude, and theme are the key elements in design today for casual dining, social drinking, and conversational coffee. Where to be, and where to be seen when having that cosmopolitan or that double-shot-grande-non-fat-no-whip-mocha-latte, are considerations when choosing a spot to meet friends, or hang out with a good book. In *Bars, Pubs, Cafés,* we'll take a look at the more exciting spaces created by designers, architects, and proprietors that will include restaurant and hotel bars, cocktail lounges, night clubs, coffee houses, and cafés. We're looking at style, elegance, whimsy, and charm to lead the way.

Whether in Toronto, Tokyo, San Francisco, or London, style is the paramount objective, so we've organized this social tour by visual theme. Designers' imaginations really let loose in "Fantasia," which looks at places bursting with decoration and ornamentation, from cartoon to coastal themes. Far from the chintz-filled ladies' spaces or too-dark dives, "Grape, Grain, Leaf, Bean" represents sophisticated pouring spots.

INTRODUCTION

Julie D. Taylor

"Glamour Days" will take you back to that golden age of Hollywood, when the elegance of a cigarette holder and martini were beyond this world (Dahling). "Contemporary Comfort" covers clean, contemporary spaces that are filled with texture and calm.

"Art Attack" exhibits new talents and old masters alike. "Minimal Moments" are had at modern, elegant establishments where the decor is sparse, yet inviting. And finally, we'll soar to "Jetsonia," where the sky's the limit.

The universal appeal of these spaces is evident, not only by the broad range of styles, but by the settings as well—from downtown San Francisco to the Red Sea of Israel. I also realized how much interest there was in this topic when so many friends and acquaintances volunteered to be my "research assistants" on this project. To all of them—and to all of you—I raise a glass in toast to fine design and elegant living. Cheers!

The far reaches of imagination are mined for spaces that evoke other worlds. High concepts and intense decorative schemes bring to mind dreams and hallucinations alike. In these rooms, no detail is overlooked—hardware, tiles, lights, walls, and ceilings are infused with the design theme. Water is stylishly displayed at Potion, whose bubbly blue environment intoxicates the eyes. Marine forms abound at the underwater haven of Red

FANTASIA

Sea Star. The netherworld is evoked at Le Bar Bat, whose Gothic trappings are both spooky and seductive. Amnesia lives up to its name—banishing cares in an unforgettable design. The imagination runs deep at the ultra-animated Iridium, which is clearly influenced by baby-boomer cartoon watching; the walls vibrate, furniture seems to dance and run, and lights play a perpetual game of hide-and-seek.

OPPOSITE: A highly stylized gargoyle bat is the macabre, high-tech mascot for the bar.

BELOW: Cobalt blue glass filters light from outside and sets the cool night tones against deep blood hues of the floor.

PHOTOGRAPHY: NORMAN MCGRATH

Le Bar Bat CENTRAL, HONG KONG

Hong Kong's nighthawks enjoy Le Bar Bat, with its visually rich, exquisite details that open the eyes of any blind reveler. Tony Chi & Associates themes this nightspot around gothic hauntings of bats and vampires. Rather than imposing a scary and alien view, the design is meant to seduce visitors into feeling at home. Intimate seating areas are delineated by high-back, fortress-like booths. Pony-skin wall covering is layered in patches, recalling castle masonry. Kilim rugs that don the floors are also used as thick, dramatic curtains. Slick, rich wood paneling and barstools bring in contemporary elements. Dramatic and specific, the use of lighting creates a rhythm through the space, leading visitors deeper into the den. Narrow spots cast an eerie glow on gargoyle statues, further heightening their macabre charm. The ceiling drips with deep, bloody red plaster embellished with gold leaf. The feeling of eternal night is teased by the use of glowing blue glass windows, which color the light from outside and seem to implore the impending dawn.

OPPOSITE: Hanging Kilim rugs frame the slick wood bar haunted by gargoyles in niches.

RIGHT: Arcs and arabesques of metal support cocktail tables among a variety of animated bar stools and seats.

Potion NEW YORK, NEW YORK

Elixirs, "love formulas," and heady mixtures entice visitors to Potion, an Upper West Side lounge designed by Robert D. Henry Architects. The pulsing blue interiors practically spill out onto the street through large illuminated windows inset with continual bubbles. Intoxication is immediate upon entering the azure, watery world of swirling banquettes, suede upholstery, and intimate lighting. Original brick walls were left in place for contrast of materials and a down-to-earth feeling. Sensual red is introduced in the casual sofa area and in the basket-weave wall and ceiling structure. The hand-polished, stainless-steel bar is faced in luminous iridescent blue recycled mosaic tile, and meanders around, creating pockets for intimate conversation, or broader spaces for group gatherings. Along the back-lit bar, colorful spirits show the raw materials of the unusual potion drinks made by a unique system of layering ingredients. The artful drinks are dramatically presented along the fiber-optic–lit bar to further highlight their sparkling contents. The mystery of potion is heightened in the detail behind the bar, where translucence and opacity come together in a beautiful alchemical mixture.

ABOVE: Watery window walls bubble up along Columbus Avenue.

OPPOSITE: Colorful potions are served along the fiber-optic–lit, stainless-steel bar.

PHOTOGRAPHY: PAUL WARCHOL (UNLESS NOTED)

ABOVE: Sensual swirls are carved in velvet banquette backs that surround clear-glass tables with carved edges for added sparkle.

RIGHT: Recycled blue mosaic tile faces the broad sweep of the bar, contrasting the sinuous line of banquettes.

OPPOSITE: A laminated basket-weave screen defines a casual sofa area next to the hand-burnished metal partition.

RIGHT: Translucent bar inset lends a mysterious glow from behind.
(Photo: Jimmy Cohrssen)

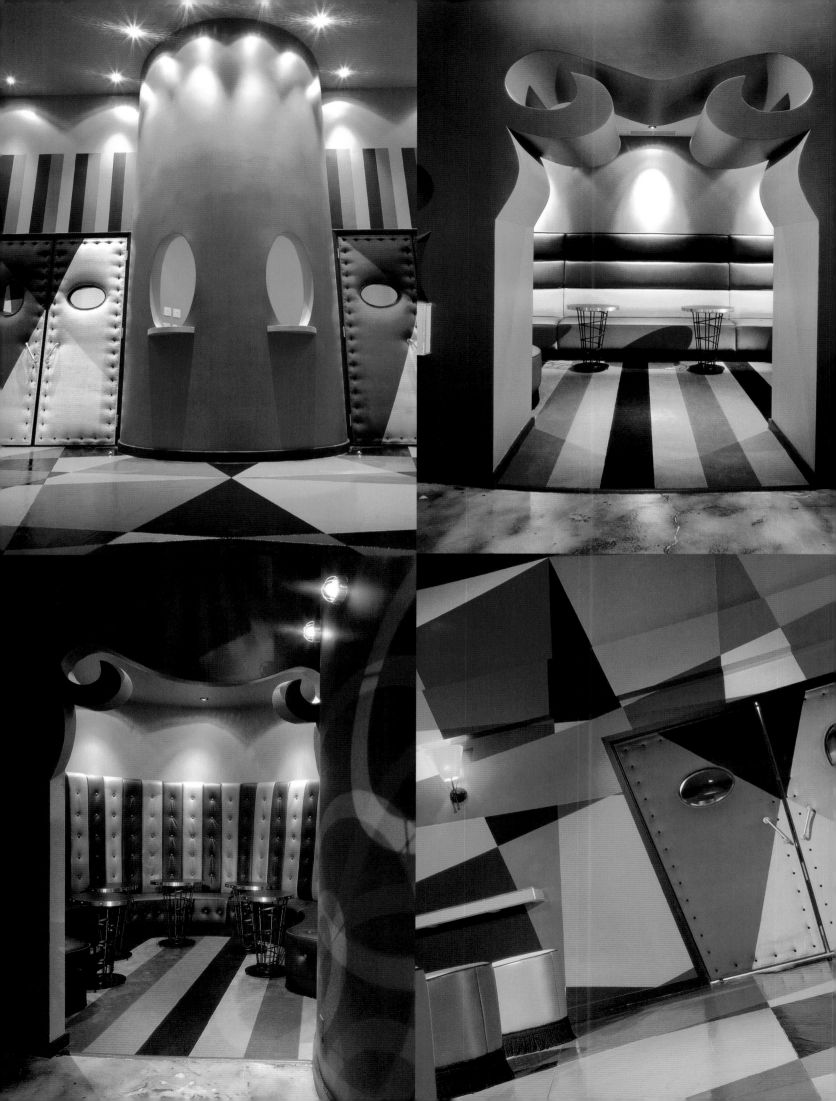

Amnesia TORONTO, ONTARIO, CANADA

Once inside the kaleidoscopic wonderland Amnesia, all troubles are forgotten. II by IV Design Associates creates a space true to its name, causing amnesia from the everyday. Set within a former tile showroom in a strip mall, this sprawling club uses off-scale dimensions, exaggerated shapes, and saturated color in a mixed homage to "Alice Through the Looking Glass, the Electric Kool-Aid Acid Test, the Joker, Licorice Allsorts, Jelly Beans, and Slinky Toys," according to the designers. One enters through this looking glass by a series of doors and gateways to the circular cashier station reminiscent of an old-time amusement arcade ticket booth. Large doors on either side continue the distorted, circus images with bright upholstery and geometric cut-outs. The harlequin-inspired patterns are bold and simple, energized by their size and vibrant colors. Private lounges are introduced by sculptural, three-foot-thick walls, and delineated by contrasting color combinations: blue and teal, orange and fuchsia, green and yellow. Floors correspond in color in deep tones painted on concrete and topped with clear iridescent epoxy. Easy to get out of hand, the designers remember how to combine broad decorative elements in an unforgettable way.

OPPOSITE (clockwise from top left): An old-time ticket booth welcomes visitors bent on forgetting their cares. Fanciful cornices are carved from three-foot-thick walls that define a series of separate lounges. Kaleidoscopic imagery plays sight-perception games with visitors. The mottled cement floor contrasts with a series of tight stripe patterns.

ABOVE: A dizzying array of vibrant color and shape creates a magical, through-the-looking-glass feeling.

PHOTOGRAPHY: DAVID WHITTAKER

ABOVE LEFT: Vertical and horizontal stripes of carpeting and upholstery in candy colors play against swirling tables and moldings.

ABOVE RIGHT: Studded silver and reflective glass are cool spots for eye-rest within this color-block world.

BELOW: Abstracted musical notations introduce the performing arts themes.

OPPOSITE: Each surface is alive with music and movement, with pirouetting ceiling spiral and tap-dancing bar stool legs.

PHOTOGRAPHY: ANDREW GARN

Iridium NEW YORK, NEW YORK

"Gotta dance!" Iridium shouts its intentions to the world. A quick *jeté* away from New York's Lincoln Center for the Performing Arts, which houses two ballet companies, Iridium is a pre- and post-performance inspiration for audience and performers alike. Jordan Mozer & Associates infuses dance, music, rhythm, and delight in every tile, table, light, seat, and space by answering the question: "What would music look like as it began to solidify?" From the overture, the facade is roofed with copper spirals derived from the sensual violin. Columns are inspired by Russian Constructivist ballets; cabinets seem to pirouette and shyly take a bow; music drips from saxophone lighting fixtures; chairs wear toe shoes and legwarmers; and settees perform beautiful *pas de deux*. Like a fine symphony, these extraordinary combinations are woven within a logical structure.

ABOVE: A shy "ballerina" trips the light fantastic.

ABOVE RIGHT: Cocktail tables accommodate larger pre- and post-theater groups.

OPPOSITE: Stylish chairs sport dance shoes and leg-warmers.

OPPOSITE: Whimsical jellyfish bar stools give patrons the further feeling of being part of the Red Sea as they gaze through the windows onto coral reefs.

BELOW: Red Sea Star is 350 feet (1050 meters) off the Eilat shore and 20 feet (6 meters) below the surface of the water.

PHOTOGRAPHY: ALBI SERFATY

Red Sea Star EILAT, ISRAEL

Submerged 20 feet (6 meters) below the surface, Red Sea Star by Aqua Creations is an underwater fantasy whose creativity is as deep as the ocean itself. The designer crafted each element, from lighting fixtures in sea-life forms to a *faux*-barnacle–faced bar front. Sixty-two windows and skylights (wouldn't they really be "sealights"?) allow guests to gaze upon the rich coral reefs and exotic fish. The intense blueness of the ocean is complemented inside by warm tones in the colors of the sea, such as coral, sand, and ochre. Sea forms are abstracted in the dramatic ceiling lighting fixtures, whose amber glow is reflected in the mirrored sand floors and polished coral tables. Table bases are sinuous floral forms, as are the whimsical jelly-fish bar stools. "I wanted to balance the experience of floating weightlessly in the water with the stable feeling of being safe on shore," says designer Ayala Serfaty. Metal screens in vegetation filigreed patterns separate tables and reflect throughout the space. Organically shaped columns are covered with tactile fabric material similar to Aqua Creations' famous lamps. Like the schools of fish swimming outside the windows, the design comprises several varying elements that repeat throughout the space to create similar patterns—and great delight.

ABOVE: Sinuous, organic columns correspond with the variety of wavy curves and shapes throughout the space.

OPPOSITE, ABOVE: Lights, furniture, and surfaces are imbued with fanciful sea-like forms.

OPPOSITE, BELOW: Glowing amber lights seem to emerge from the deep-sea darkness.

FOLLOWING SPREAD: *Faux* barnacles cover the bar front. "Sealights" give total views of the Red Sea at Eilat bay.

Settings for specific beverages often bring design tropes quickly to mind: wood with wine, brick with ale, chintz with tea. The spaces here reach beyond the clichés into lifestyle, atmosphere, and comfort. Wine bars remain elegant and wood-clad, but—as at Hayes and Vine—are also light, contemporary, and sophisticated with rich colors of Bordeaux, cabernet, and sauterne. Far from

GRAPE, GRAIN, LEAF, BEAN

the frills of English ladies' teatime, The Tea Box is of Eastern extraction as is Cha Yu; both are housed in Takashimaya stores. Donut King gives a cheery wake-up call to coffee and donuts (yes they are good for you!). A down-home Creole look resonates in Mud Bug's lively interior. Whether you fancy a brew of tea or grain, or the sweet juice of the grape, you can find just the right place to hang your hat and wet your whistle.

OPPOSITE: Billowing silk ceiling panels, asymmetrical cut-out walls, and natural upholstery form an abstract tableau.

BELOW: Takashimaya glows on Fifth Avenue in Manhattan. (Photo: Julie D. Taylor)

PHOTOGRAPHY: PETER MARGONELLI (UNLESS NOTED)

The Tea Box NEW YORK, NEW YORK

When the upscale Japanese department store Takashimaya came to New York, it settled, appropriately, on Fifth Avenue. The Tea Box restaurant and retail space is elegantly designed by CR Studio Architects in a space that was previously designated for storage and mechanical areas. With the constraints of low ceilings and no windows, the designers instilled a light, soothing color palette and clever design solutions to create an inviting space. Using a "walled garden" metaphor, seating and retail spaces are separated by low partitions that gently delineate each area while allowing a cohesive flow of space. The walls are finished in subtle patterns and textures that recall burnished silver and traditional gold-leafing. The central space is organized by a series of elegant silk ceiling panels lit from behind to give the room both height and a sense of lightness.

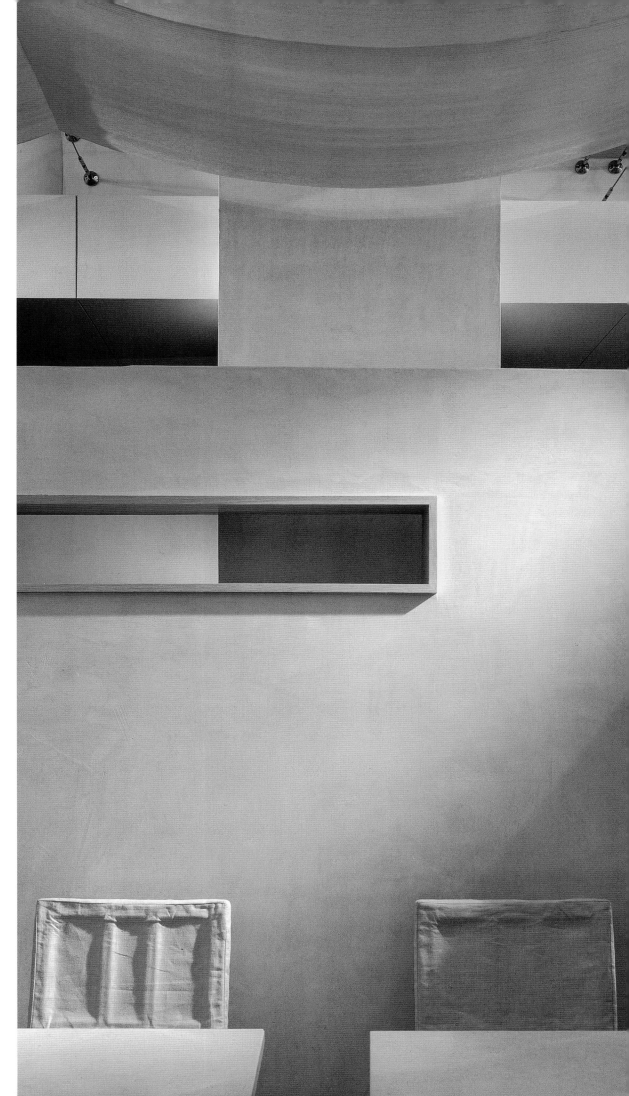

OPPOSITE: Metallic walls punctuated with intense lights shimmer against wood and steel furniture.

RIGHT: Designed around a walled garden motif, partitions are given various surfaces of wood, wallcovering, and fabric.

OPPOSITE (clockwise from top): Open box shelves show tea in both traditional and contemporary containers. Tea-cup graphics line the long banquette wall that leads to a curved seating area. A curved booth the color of green tea supports an illuminated display wall. Keeping with the department-store ambiance, the bright retail space invites visitors.

BELOW: Takashimaya Department Store in Tokyo is a glittering contemporary high-rise.

PHOTOGRAPHY: ALAN CHAN

Cha Yu—Alan Chan Tea Room

TOKYO, JAPAN

Located on the sixth floor of the Takashimaya Department Store in Shinjuku-ku, Tokyo, Cha Yu—Alan Chan Tea Room is a joint venture between the JapanGreenTea Company and Alan Chan Design Company. As designer and owner, Chan's hand is seen throughout the project—from interiors and finishes to corporate identity and product packaging. Finding inspiration in East-West combinations of design, he fashions the Chinese characters of Cha Yu (meaning "the language of tea") into the shape of a traditional tea cup for the logo, but lets slip the English phonetic of the name like escaped vapor. The retail space is bright, in keeping with the department store corridors, yet leads to the darker-toned tea room. The long seating area features tightly-wrapped seats along a shoji-screen–inspired wall on one side, with a banquette wall showing more graphic tea cups on the other. A curved wooden wall punctuated with light and Chinese objects rises above straight banquette seating upholstered in the color of green tea. The gaps and cantilevers of the display wall hint at the work of Frank Lloyd Wright, who was, in turn, influenced by Japanese patterning and construction, bringing the East-West connections full circle.

BELOW: Wine-label–like sign in friendly calligraphy sets a neighborhood tone.

OPPOSITE: Semi-circular tables come together to complete the circular geometry of the chairs against the low-slung bench.

PHOTOGRAPHY: SHARON RISENDORPH

Hayes and Vine Wine Bar

SAN FRANCISCO, CALIFORNIA

John Lum Architecture replaces pseudo-Victorian law offices with the elegant Hayes and Vine Wine Bar for busy professionals in the cultural center of San Francisco. The sophisticated space appeals to opera and symphony patrons, as well as to the art crowd visiting neighborhood galleries and museums. The space is organized by a curving wine-colored wall that creates an intimate room for wine tastings. The curvaceous, white onyx bar is uplit in the center of the room, giving a luminous, liquid glow. A custom steel glass rack artfully displays the variety of glassware needed for the appropriate connoisseurship of wines. French salon seating is paired with low banquettes with removable bolsters, all upholstered in lush combinations of crushed velvet, stripes, harlequin patterns, and stars. The earthly colors of wine complement clear maple paneling and furniture. The green-stained floor lends a vineyard quality to the space.

OPPOSITE: A private booth, sensually upholstered in rich concord-grape velvet, evokes the Dyonisian delights of the vine.

ABOVE LEFT: The verdant floor is a perfect backdrop to wine-red walls and jaunty geometric furniture.

ABOVE: A curving slab of white onyx sits atop the marble bar set with star-upholstered stools and reflects the custom-designed glass rack.

OPPOSITE: The large beer-dispensing refrigerator in the background is bolstered by a stainless-steel tower that will be filled with beer cans from around the world.

BELOW: The Can logo is artfully displayed on the front window, through which the beer tubes are evident, yet mysterious.

PHOTOGRAPHY: RENE CHAVANNE

Can LONDON, ENGLAND

Going from conception to completion in only six months, Can represents a way of working, thinking, and socializing for the new millennium. Designed by the young firm known as Jump, Can is the first in a chain of beer bars that is a vast departure from brick-lined pubs. With a futuristic, bright, shiny interior of chrome and glass, Can is sparsely furnished to keep patrons active and in touch with each other. A huge, custom-designed refrigerator dispenses brews from all over the world to thirsty beer-lovers. When empty, the cans are fed into one of four large pneumatic tubes or "suckers" that lead to the basement-level crushers that prepare the cans for recycling. In this way, patrons actively participate in the recycling. They even get a glimpse of the can traveling through the tubes from the glass floor, or from the windowed restrooms.

ABOVE: Keeping things minimal, the basement level houses patron lockers, restrooms, and automatic vending machines for snacks and novelty items.

OPPOSITE, ABOVE: The picture window in the restroom gives a view of the cans traveling through pneumatic tubes on their way to the crusher.

OPPOSITE, BELOW: Pneumatic tubes, or "suckers," take empty cans down to the recycling center.

OPPOSITE: Racing memorabilia in the bar keep patrons interested in the past and present of horseracing.

BELOW: Built to look as though it evolved over time, the exterior is a combination of diner, shack, and stable.

PHOTOGRAPHY: TIM LONG

Mud Bug OTB CHICAGO, ILLINOIS

Proving that class, fun, and zip can be interjected into any space with a keen design sense, Aumiller Youngquist Architecture gives an upscale tone to Mud Bug Off Track Betting facility. It's the first high-concept OTB site of its kind, and it's situated in a sophisticated, trendy area on Chicago's near north side. Engaging patrons in the concept, of course, is what makes a difference between a quick-exchange, and a lingering customer. "Mud Bug" is an old, affectionate term for Louisiana-born, back-stretch racetrack workers, many of whom would spend summers at Illinois racetracks. Given its origins, a Cajun flair is added in sound, color, and celebratory feeling. Racing memorabilia recalls a livelier at-track experience, with jockeys' "silks" hanging from the walls and photos and cards imbedded in the bar. Television monitors keep patrons up-to-date on the live action. Purposely mismatched barstools line the central bar. The space is designed to look like a series of interconnected buildings, giving it the feeling of evolving over time. To heighten the time element, recycled building materials are used when possible, and new elements are *faux* finished to appear aged. Each "building" houses a different function, such as bar, dining, lounge, and individual areas for handicappers. It's a place the Mud Bugs could have long called their home away from home.

OPPOSITE: Mismatched chairs and tables lend the feeling of a neighborhood bar that evolves with its clientele.

ABOVE: Recycled building materials were used where possible; newer materials were finished to give the look of a casual, lived-in hangout.

BELOW: Animated graphics update and enliven the humble donut shop genre.

OPPOSITE: Donut art and fresh flowers are unexpected touches that add sophistication.

FOLLOWING SPREAD: Bold stripes, crisp design, and donut-inspired furniture add a sunshiny feeling to the fast-food space.

PHOTOGRAPHY: RION RIZZO

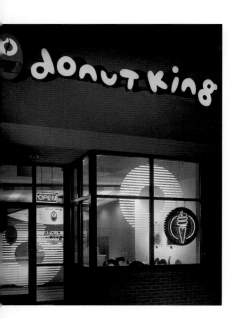

Donut King ATLANTA, GEORGIA

Bringing class and pizzazz to the humble donut is the goal of Donut King's owners and Lorenc/Yoo Design, which creates a clean, upscale, workable prototype design for the franchise. Obviously a place to catch a quick twist and cup of joe on the way to work, Donut King would not succumb to the expected low-rent look of a typical American donut shop. Using bright colors, whimsical design, and unexpected touches (fresh flowers!), Donut King reigns supreme. From the exterior, chunky animated signage brings a smile to passers-by. Bold graphics continue inside for the striped patterns in the floors and ceilings that are also echoed in custom donut art. Extending the irresistible theme are the donut-shaped chairs and tables. "Like sprinkles on a vanilla-frosted cruller," say the designers, "most of the experience is just for fun."

The sheen on Jean Harlow's satin dress. The play of light and shadow in a George Hurrell portrait. Pure, movie-star glamour adds appeal to A Bar, attracting sophisticated crowds. Using luxurious materials, such as velvet and silk, etched glass, and plenty of shine and glitter, designers create glamorous wonderlands where patrons sip their elegant martinis, and re-live a glorious past. Glamour comes in various guises, from the total

GLAMOUR DAYS

silver fantasy of Mercury, to the sparkling jewel tones of Stardust-Sangu. Many of today's designers are finding glamour in a fresh, contemporary mode by using clear, clean materials—with just a hint of glimmer—that can be found at the Rendezvous Lounge and The Hotel. Fantasy and reality converge in these high-concept spaces, some faintly reminiscent of old movie sets, others catering to today's busy professionals, who desire a little star treatment after a long day.

A Bar SANTA FE, NEW MEXICO

Glamour and style are paramount at Andrew Altchek's A Bar, a sophisticated showplace for stylish furnishings, dramatic lighting, intriguing art, and new jazz artists. Almost generic, stencil-like exterior signage belies a much more fanciful interior that welcomes visitors with dramatic etched glass, sculptural furniture, and plush upholstery. Using jazz-age–inspired design motifs, A Bar almost looks like a renovation from speakeasy days, yet is a newly designed space. The lighting is dramatic, setting a mood of intrigue. Burgundy-colored damask walls are uplit from behind plush banquettes, and perky table lamps resemble cocktail shakers with shades. Three custom-designed chandeliers are highly sculptural, adding an artistic touch to the setting. Likewise, photographer David Levinthal's lush and mysterious mental landscapes featuring cowboys and bathing beauties add intrigue and elegance.

OPPOSITE: The multi-tiered bar features *faux*-leopard upholstery on seat backs and black leather on the chair seats.

ABOVE RIGHT: Given the almost generic signage, lush interiors are a surprise.

FOLLOWING SPREAD: An altar to the spirits, the glass and stainless steel bar features back-lit, sand-blasted reliefs of sexy celestial gods.

PHOTOGRAPHY: PETER VITALE

OPPOSITE: Original David Levinthal photographs depict bathing beauties and cowboys.

ABOVE LEFT: Sexy and sensual shapes abound in the design, which appears as a renovated interior of a 1930s nightclub, yet is completely new construction.

ABOVE: Three custom light fixtures add drama and art.

Mercury SAN FRANCISCO, CALIFORNIA

Temperatures rise when entering this ultra-hot, two-level restaurant designed by Fun Display. The designers describe it as "an amalgam of chic and retro-chic elements." Lush velvets co-exist with shiny vinyls, giving a delirious mood of mixed emotions. Silver, white, and black are the only colors in this sparkling world, where the mirrored walls and ceilings are infused with bubbles. Traditional elements are updated: velvet button-upholstery is used unconventionally on all sides of the white-tiled wall opening; slipper chairs are upholstered in vinyl. Even the glittery deer head—a humorous reference to traditional bars—is silver-coated, bringing to mind the Warhol Factory, where everyone was a star (if only for 15 minutes).

ABOVE: The curtain opens on a silvery entrance.

OPPOSITE: Bubbles in the glass walls and ceilings set the mood for a cocktail lounge replete with silver-upholstered seating.

PHOTOGRAPHY: CESAR RUBIO

OPPOSITE: Floor-to-ceiling upholstered vinyl in mottled black and
white is framed by elegant, demure
curtains.

RIGHT: The multi-level space changes
quickly—true to its name—from bar to
lounge to full-scale dining.

OPPOSITE: Oversized porthole windows open to sky-high views from the lounge/restaurant, which is situated between two skyscrapers.

BELOW: Dark gives way to bright starry white at the dramatic entrance high above Osaka.

PHOTOGRAPHY: NACASA & PARTNERS

Stardust-Sangu
OSAKA, JAPAN

Situated on the top floor, spanning two high-rise towers in downtown Osaka, Stardust-Sangu lives up to its name. Interspace Time designs a powerful and theatrical cocktail lounge that emphasizes the sparkling views 39 stories above the ground. The dramatic contemporary design is both minimal and lush, with the use of deep woods, velvets, and glimmering chrome. Block-patterned quilted walls offset gleaming white-tiled floors. Warm tones give way to fiery red in the Stardust Live Lounge, where padded walls are repeated in jewel tones of red and purple. The entry-way sports zodiac symbols, reminding visitors of the constellations, and just how close to the heavens they are.

RIGHT: The Live Lounge offers music
and drama in deep jewel tones of red
and purple in alternating upholstery
and padded walls.

OPPOSITE: Black walls and red lighting
are reflected and refracted, along with
signs of the zodiac.

Rendezvous Lounge and Aft Atrium

CELEBRITY CRUISES MERCURY

Shelton, Mindel & Associates' design for the Rendezvous Lounge and Aft Atrium of Celebrity Cruises Mercury recalls the high-glamour days of ocean travel. The Aft Atrium, within a towering teak column, is a three-story lounge and champagne bar that bubbles over in exuberant design. Champagne bubbles are portrayed in back-lit, etched-glass walls and blue-and-grey carpeting. Lights within the column carry on the metaphor. Leather club chairs surround round glass tables that further the bubbly motif. An exuberant Sol Lewit mural extends the full height with color and brio. The more intimately scaled Rendezvous Lounge features sensually undulating banquettes paired with architectural seating in deep blues and reds. The round cocktail tables as in the Aft Atrium are also included, as well as materials such as leather, steel, and glass. Free-floating, semi-circular banquettes with steel and glass privacy panels are intimate spaces for gatherings.

ABOVE: The colorful Sol Lewit mural spans the three-story space with brilliant hues contrasting the subtle colors of wood and steel.

OPPOSITE: Inset lights sparkle throughout the three-story, teak-clad cylinder, echoing etched-glass bubbles in the walls.

FOLLOWING SPREAD: (Left page) Architecturally inspired red chairs contrast to the flowing blue banquettes. (Right page) The long, sensual curve of banquettes is echoed in the metal and wood ceiling pattern.

PHOTOGRAPHY: MICHAEL MORAN

OPPOSITE: (Clockwise from top left) Down to every detail, The Hotel provides custom-designed place settings for a complete, seamless experience. Over-scaled porthole windows are emphasized by the geometric shapes of furniture in the hotel lobby. An assortment of glass gendant lamps adorns the ceiling. A fanciful pouf adds drama and humor to the lobby lounge; its fresh foliage is subtle contrast to the jungle-inspired drapery.

BELOW: Recast as The Hotel, the landmark Tiffany building in Miami retains its original beacon signage.

PHOTOGRAPHY: TODD EBERLE

The Hotel MIAMI BEACH, FLORIDA

If the name Tiffany doesn't state glamour, we don't know what does. The formerly-named Tiffany hotel in Miami's tony South Beach is renamed simply The Hotel (due to copyright battles with the *other* Tiffany), and elegantly redesigned by Todd Oldham. Known for years more as a young, upstart fashion designer, Oldham brings his penchant for color and pattern to the beach-front oasis that is a favorite haunt of the young celebrity set. The building was designed in 1939 by L. Murray Dixon, and, as a condition of its landmark status, retains the 24-foot-high (7.2 meter-high) neon Tiffany sign. Oldham also retains its over-scaled porthole windows and original terrazzo lobby floor. Using the floor as inspiration, he chooses a muted jewel-tone color palette for upholstery and tile mural walls. The gentle geometry of the lobby—portrayed in the round windows and tables, and linear sofas and banquettes— is quickly offset by the fanciful poufs that bring back glory days of Florida's most sumptuous hotels in both their shape, and outrageous plants sprouting from atop. The bar area blends the two color themes of muted ochres and olives with more lively shades of blue. Again combining geometries, Oldham presents textured, round, bull's-eye seat cushions with flat, square tiles. Transforming the round bar stools to square café seats lends enough differentiation between the two spaces, which are separated by levels. A fanciful collection of glass pendant lamps hangs overhead, while the designer's touch extends even to the place settings.

OPPOSITE: Hand-cut glass and tile adorning the back wall of the café and other areas of the hotel lounge sparkle against the assortment of glass pendant lamps.

RIGHT: Bull's-eye-patterned bar stools sit perkily by the lively bar, which uses flat tile panels and the spirit bottles themselves as further decoration.

One of today's design trends is the no-trend space—a comfortable contemporary interior that takes its cues from honest use of materials and a pared-down aesthetic. These spaces create a neutral, but not boring, setting for entertaining and relaxation, as evidenced at

CONTEMPORARY COMFORT

The Edmond Meany Hotel and Bond Street. Materials are used to appeal at Sinibar, in combinations that keep color palettes monochromatic but surface interest high. Although seemingly simple, these contemporary spaces are replete with subtle detail in fabrics, wood grains, paint finishes, and furniture, such as can be experienced at Veruka and Nic's.

OPPOSITE: Rich patterns of spices within shadowboxes bring Oriental flavors to visual life.

BELOW: Dusty olive and khaki exterior shows the colors of explorers' garb.

PHOTOGRAPHY: DAVID GLOMB

Sinibar CHICAGO, ILLINOIS

Deep tones and scents of the spice trade waft through the imagination where glimpsing Sinibar, designed by Insite West. A mixture of exotic travel memories—from Mexico to Africa, to China and back—this den is a world-tour of materials. Sculptural ancient Chinese tree roots act as table bases and lamps. Wood panels are carved with tribal African motifs, and kubba cloths are used for draperies and wall hangings. Natural rattan, linen, sisal, and rope materials are used on oversized, yet tailored, chairs and barstools. Shadow boxes of dried botanical mixes, including cinnamon sticks and chestnuts, grace the Mayan red walls behind the limestone, metal, and wood-paneled bar.

OPPOSITE: Oversized hassocks double
as tables in natural, nubby material,
surrounded by rattan chairs.

ABOVE: African-inspired materials
frame the doorway.

OPPOSITE: Cinnamon-colored slip-covers hold the warm glow of mustard and cardamom-colored upholstery.

ABOVE: Linen-covered barstools face the Mayan red bar accented with Mexican water jugs and rawhide shaded lamps.

Veruka NEW YORK, NEW YORK

Urban, downtown loft living is the impetus for Veruka, where designer David Schefer creates a series of residential vignettes. Rustic and refined elements are explored through existing brick walls and nubby textiles contrasted with woven and folded steel for an industrial aesthetic. Wide-plank flooring is inset with illuminated panels in shapes echoing clever cut-outs in two-toned upholstered chairs. Saturated colors add warmth and depth in fabrics and multi-hued wall collages.

ABOVE: A secret, speakeasy ambiance is emphasized by minimal signage and red velvet curtains. (Photo: Julie D. Taylor)

OPPOSITE: Exposed metal pipes and steel bar are softened by rose-toned fabrics and floor.

PHOTOGRAPHY: DAVID M. JOSEPH (UNLESS NOTED)

ABOVE: Steel is used for decorative effect in woven screen patterns.

RIGHT: Positive and negative slats of space and light create a pattern leading to an artist's color-block paper wall collage.

OPPOSITE: Minimal color works to great effect at the sushi bar, where sight-lines are kept level.

BELOW: The inconspicuous entrance states the restaurant's Japanese flavor in the red O. (Photo: Julie D. Taylor)

PHOTOGRAPHY: DAVID M. JOSEPH (unless noted)

Bond Street   NEW YORK, NEW YORK

Named for its Lower East Side Manhattan location, Bond Street by Studio Gaia is a serene secret among the downtown scene. This sushi spot infuses sparse Eastern asceticism with warm richness. Traditional shoji screen ornamentation is used on windows and ceiling grids. A long sushi bar is inviting with low-back stools in dimpled leather. Neutral grey and natural wood respect materials and the elements. The dining area is created by a series of small lounge-like niches with high-grain dark wood tables set among banquettes or leather booths. Dotting the aisles are low stools requiring the grace and agility of a Geisha.

OPPOSITE: Dark shoji-like ceiling detail is repeated subtly behind the booths for added privacy.

RIGHT: Minimal seating requires concentration and agility in a sparse setting.

BELOW: The original chevron design is retained, and new graphics are influenced by the 1930s architect's signage.

OPPOSITE: Custom-designed wall sconces bend toward seating arrangements and are sparklingly reflected in full-height framed mirrors.

PHOTOGRAPHY: FARSHID ASSASSI

The Edmond Meany Hotel

SEATTLE, WASHINGTON

Designed in 1931 by Robert C. Reamer as an example of Art Deco architecture, The Edmond Meany Hotel had undergone several unfortunate facelifts and name changes prior to NBBJ's current renovation. Restoring the building to its former glory gives the site its original name (after a popular professor at the University of Washington), materials, and striking style. The original lobby plan is restored, with a large atrium for elegant meetings among the tinkling of piano keys. Previously hidden columns and terrazzo floors are brought to new life. Contemporary furniture designed with Hollywood Golden Era intention spot the lobby. Newly designed column lights curve gracefully toward drink and game tables, almost aching to hear private conversations.

One part of the ground floor is reserved for the small Eddie's Newscafé. An intimate space meant to attract hotel guests and neighborhood residents, the café offers coffees, magazines, snacks, cigars, and a gentle, easy place for contemplation or conversation. Keeping with the original Art Deco design of the building, custom metal screens and railings use design motifs from the '30s, and antique posters add bold graphics. The designers also took liberties in adding contemporary materials and design, such as concrete counter tops and perforated brass bar front. With the mixture of old and new, Professor Meany himself would have been comfortable at his namesake café.

ABOVE: New metalwork is designed to correspond to the building's Art Deco origins.

RIGHT: Golden hues and mahogany railing soften concrete and steel materials.

OPPOSITE: Mixing old and new, concrete coffee bar and antique posters combine for a lively ambience.

OPPOSITE: Industrial resin tops the bar, while natural rattan and cherry continue a cocktail mixture of materials.

BELOW: Jigsaw-puzzle-shaped custom barstools and chairs have an animated and modern feeling.

PHOTOGRAPHY: DOUGLAS HILL

Nic's BEVERLY HILLS, CALIFORNIA

Nic's—a cool, new martini lounge—rises from Unruh Boyer on the spot where Dean Martin used to have nightly Italian dinners. The place is transformed into a comfortable, contemporary space with color-block patterns and custom furniture styled somewhere in between '50s and '90s sensibilities. The large bar is topped with resin material, but supported by a combination of cherry with rattan inserts, giving a mixed industrial and natural look. Barstools have a jigsaw-puzzle look and are topped with contrasting green and black pie-patterned *faux* leather. Origami-type lanterns hang from above. Banquette seating features light emanating from the top of cherry-wood wainscoting. Velvet upholstery in alternating green and purple grape colors echoes the block patterns of the vine- and olive- green carpeting. Cocktail tables are faced with resin, as is the bar. Curved booths define the dining area with vine-patterned tapestry upholstery. Jaunty chairs are inspired by Modern French designer Jean Prouvé, and made of plywood to complement the bar stools. A small homage to Dino—a simple shelf with a candle and fresh-daily martini—hangs where his regular table once was.

OPPOSITE: Color-block patterns are used to great effect in upholstery and carpeting. Dean Martin's photo and fresh martini hang on the wall.

BELOW: The dining room features booths upholstered in leaf-patterned fabric.

The hand and eye of an artist bring expressive life to any room—from high Renaissance to low Pop, infusing spaces with elegance and pizzazz. Art can be used literally, as with the adaptation of Raphael's famous Vatican murals, which bring a subtle, intellectual spiritualism to The Plantation Coffee & Tea Co., or by appropriating

ART ATTACK

Roy Lichtenstein–like images to lend pop and polish to Bam Wraps' fast-food joint. Specially-commissioned art fills Lot 61, a nightspot that caters to the creative cognoscenti. Art abounds at G. Point Bar, where lighting, furniture, and other design elements are sculptural and expressive. And, sometimes, a simple color makes a bold statement—see The Red Room.

The Plantation Coffee & Tea Co.
TORONTO, ONTARIO, CANADA

Although a new café in downtown Toronto, the Plantation Coffee & Tea Co. portrays an aged look, thanks to the work of Candeloro Designs. Using fresco reproductions from the Vatican, the space evokes artistic, intellectual, and spiritual countenance. On the imposing back wall, Raphael's famous "School of Athens" gathers portraits of the world's greatest philosophers, artists, and scientists. Besides a testament to knowledge and thought, the Renaissance fresco is known as a classic example of one-point perspective. The large, open space—featuring 20-foot-high (6-meter-high) ceilings and windows on three sides—maintains the warm coffee-bar feeling in its furniture and finishes. With only one solid wall in the space, the café's service bar is fashioned as a large kiosk, including product display. Colored-glass lights jut out from the kiosk top, recalling fanfare pageantry of the Renaissance.

OPPOSITE: Five different styles of chairs, plus sofas in varying upholsteries, give each area of the café an individual flavor.

ABOVE: Key details repeated from "The School of Athens" include portraits of Renaissance masters such as Bramante (left) and Michelangelo (right).

PHOTOGRAPHY: DAVID WHITTAKER

ABOVE: Fabric swags and glass down-lights add subtle color.

OPPOSITE: With only one solid wall out of four, the café's main counter is designed as a rounded kiosk.

BELOW: An imposing facade both hides and reveals secrets.

OPPOSITE: Translucent movable panels keep the space fluid and malleable to accommodate individual groups and events.

FOLLOWING SPREAD: Black and red seating is made of dense rubber, originally designed for use in psychiatric hospitals.

PHOTOGRAPHY: MICHAEL KLEINBERG

Lot 61 NEW YORK, NEW YORK

With the late '90s migration of art galleries from Manhattan's Soho to Chelsea district, Lot 61 fits into the new art-centered social scene. The former automotive repair garage is transformed by Rafael Viñoly Architects using extreme materials and contemporary art. Artists such as Damien Hirst, Jorge Pardo, and David Salle were among those commissioned to create work expressly for this sprawling, 6,000-square-foot (540-sqare-meter) bar, lounge, and private restaurant. Sliding translucent panels allow the larger space to be subdivided for individual private parties. Lending an exclusive, speakeasy flair is the brick entry wall with mysteriously tinted windows and imposing metal doors. An equally heavy steel and zinc bar is a swirling vertiginous separator between the stark geometry of the entrance and of the lounge area beyond. The simple-looking glass back bar holding bottles is transformed on the other side into a living mural of light and tone set against black and red furniture. The chunky sofas are actually rubber seating specified for extreme psychiatric wards, adding another high-tech, yet on-the-edge feeling. For a more elegant ambiance, zebra-patterned upholstery brings to mind the old El Morocco club and the swinging days of New York night life.

OPPOSITE: Hints of the old El Morocco club hark back to classic night life.

ABOVE: A grand gesture, the wavy metal bar gives a distinct sense of place and welcoming.

OPPOSITE: Laminate, linoleum, paint, and tile are used to great effect and economy in this space frequented by college students.

BELOW: The winsome look of a Lichtenstein-inspired lass from romance comics oversees the action.

FOLLOWING SPREAD: Upholstered counter and banquette seating add a more elegant flair to normal fast-food spaces.

PHOTOGRAPHY: MARK LOHMAN

Bam Wraps IRVINE, CALIFORNIA

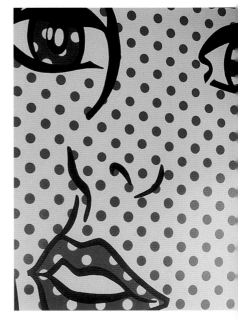

William Hefner Architect literally wraps Pop around this university café. Bam Wraps plays off artist Roy Lichtenstein's comic book–inspired style with primary colors and a "California Girl" supergraphic. Although fun and kitschy, the design is meant to bring a higher order to convenient fast food for students. The space is sparkling, with seating and counter arrangements for quick bites or lingering lunches. A primary-color palette is augmented with greens for a subliminal nod at freshness. Simple, high-traffic materials, such as embossed linoleum floor, plastic laminate, stainless steel, tile, and fiberglass fit the artful bill.

BELOW: Just a speck of blue and yellow neon is the only respite from the wild red.

OPPOSITE: A wall of mysterious red liquid is a sparkling entry to the red den.

PHOTOGRAPHY: CESAR RUBIO

The Red Room SAN FRANCISCO, CALIFORNIA

Call it crimson, scarlet, ruby, cherry, or vermilion—it's red! The Red Room by Fun Display is deeply, sanguinely saturated in its every corpuscle. One enters this den of delight through a portal of bottles filled with mysterious red liquid. This "devilishly glamorous hell bar," as the designers describe it, is moderated by an expert combination of materials, such as leather, steel, suede, and wood, giving a break to the red sea. Other textural details include Italian glass mosaic tiles, hand-carved columns, and spots of neon.

ABOVE: Bottles of red spirits create perilous walls.

LEFT: Various textures and treatments of floors, walls, and upholstery keep the saturated color from becoming too overwhelming.

RIGHT: Unsual barstools give a precarious perch to patrons

FAR RIGHT: The colors from trendy cocktails spell relief from the red.

OPPOSITE (clockwise from top left): Alternating geometric designs add life to the whimsical seating arrangements. Custom-made, steel-framed sofas sport exaggerated proportions and faux red leather. Fiber-optic bundles are used to create a sprawling sculptural art piece that illuminates the blue walls. The telecommunications tree holds computer monitors for patrons to access the Internet and games.

BELOW: Sculptural doorways hold copper-clad doors that are embossed and flamed to resemble animal skin.

PHOTOGRAPHY: LUIGI GARIGLIO

G. Point Bar   TURIN, ITALY

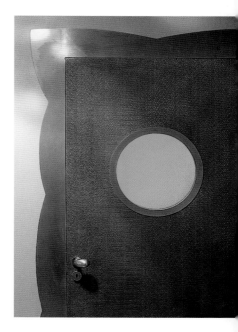

A pure, multi-media extravaganza, G. Point Bar hosts a lively crowd both day and night. Designed by Antonio Besso-Marcheis, the colorful space sports video monitors, playstations, and internet consoles for patrons to gather and while away the artful hours. Dubbed "anti-contextual" by the architect, the space is coated with blue paint and illuminated by a sprawling fiber-optic sculpture and custom-designed perforated metal sconces and pendant lights. The centerpiece is the "telecommunications tree," an imposing double column clad with oxidized copper and equipped with monitors. Along the top, it holds reflective laminate to heighten the dizzying feeling of the space. Custom café tables have single legs of tubular plumbing copper with tapered steel lugs, weighted cast-iron feet, and riveted steel tops. Swirly shapes abound in the alternating green and yellow sculptural chairs. High-back, austere sofas are covered with red *faux* leather. An industrial loft feeling is found in the wood flooring and myriad metal finishes.

OPPOSITE, FAR LEFT: Custom tables
are designed with copper piping, steel
lugs, and cast-iron feet.

OPPOSITE: Perforated copper sheeting
is used throughout for pendant and
sconce lighting.

ABOVE: Lounging options range from
café tables to austere sofas

The Zenlike quality of a sparsely designed space catalyzes conversation and contemplation. Simple minimalism is evident at Bar 89 and Warner Hollywood Commissary. Whether at a high-end jazz club, such as Shinjuku-Heichinrou, or the neighborhood fixture Delicatessen R&B, minimal design showcases the diners and the place as well as the designer's considerable

talents. When elements are stripped to their essence, only the true artist is able to handle them with such control. Pure white is given myriad shapes and styles at Eurochow. Trust in materials and space planning set these environments apart, giving patrons the freedom and openness to express themselves.

OPPOSITE: The long narrow space flows seamlessly from entrance to bar, seating areas, and upstairs intimate lounge.

BELOW: Set between two historic buildings, the bar appears as an industrial skeleton—simultaneously a foundation and simplification of the past.

PHOTOGRAPHY: ANTOINE BOOTZ

Bar 89 NEW YORK, NEW YORK

Nestled among the historic Cast Iron District of Downtown Manhattan's trendy Soho area is the clean, clear design of Bar 89 by Ogawa/Depardon. A strong iron and glass facade entrance initiates the theme of transparency, which is continued in the skylights and lack of boundaries among bar, cocktail, and dining areas. The industrial look of the entrance heightens the transparent effects by acting almost as a skeleton of the historic buildings on either side. The double-height space accentuates the long, narrow former parking lot site by dominating one whole side with the hemispherical bar. The curve of the bar is echoed in the hostess wall at front and the stairway leading to the upper lounge in the rear. Bar 89 takes the minimal tenets of simplicity of space and materials to heart.

FAR LEFT: Skylighting brings additional lightness and airy feeling to the narrow space.

CENTER: The play between indoor and outdoor space is evident through the massive entrance way, which acts as a two-way mirror looking into the bar and then out to the street life beyond.

BELOW: Curves gently offset the strict angular geometry of the façade.

BELOW: A formerly "anonymous stucco box" was reconfigured and clad in gleaming white ceramic tile.

OPPOSITE: Lightness and transparency are accented by an abundant use of glass and light woods.

PHOTOGRAPHY: LORCAN O'HERLIHY/CONRAD JOHNSON

Delicatessen R&B SANTA MONICA, CALIFORNIA

A deceptively simple, small box of a building was renovated from an office space to a comfortable, casual café by Lorcan O'Herlihy Architects. Situated in front of a small motel, the now gleaming-bright tile building serves hotel guests as well as patrons of this busy main street. For drama and effect along the active street, the architect raised the roof-line parapet, adding a patinated brass canopy to announce both the name and entrance of the deli. An additional eating area on the side gives the minimal space maximum usage. Inside, white tile flooring is punctuated with Piet Mondrian–like patterning for added interest and geometry. Seating, shelving, and the central elliptical storage/display unit are in tones of light, neutral wood, and accented by metal tables and fixtures.

OPPOSITE: A narrow patinated bronze canopy accents a small outdoor eating area.

ABOVE: The flooring takes its decorative cues from the primary-colored geometric paintings of Mondrian.

Shinjuku-Heichinrou TOKYO, JAPAN

Although clean in its solid geometry, the sky-high Shinjuku-Heichinrou is lush in its materials and lighting. The design team from Interspace Time departs from the conventional design of Chinese restaurants in favor of a more contemporary style suited to the urban setting and sophisticated clientele of dignitaries, entertainers, and professionals. Upon entering the space, the maitre d' operates an electronic rust-coated steel door to expose the lobby lounge and bar with a panoramic view 54 floors above downtown Tokyo. Low-profile custom seating and tables aid in the unobstructed view. Although sleek and sophisticated, the space is constructed primarily of recycled materials: screens are made from car metal parts; discarded lumber and old machines become furniture; paper, glass, and stone are remade into building materials. Adding to these indigenous Japanese materials is new, imported French limestone.

ABOVE: The dramatically lit entry way gives off a sophisticated, austere air.

OPPOSITE: Panoramic views of Tokyo are unencumbered by the low-profile furniture, as well as by privacy screens made from recycled car parts.

PHOTOGRAPHY: NACASA & PARTNERS

ABOVE: Steel grates at once shield
and reveal stunning views.

OPPOSITE: Pin-pointed spot lighting
accents spaces of dining, lounging,
and entrance.

OPPOSITE, FAR RIGHT: The spot-lit cor-
ridor is lined with limestone walls
sandblasted with calligraphy, and inset
with oxidized metal door.

BELOW: Heavy steel fins slicing through the building's facade play counterpoint to the openness of glass doors and windows.

OPPOSITE: The host station acts as a microcosm of structural and decorative details in its use of glass, metal, and natural wood.

FOLLOWING SPREAD: Issues of transparency and fenestration are artfully addressed.

PHOTOGRAPHY: ERICH ANSEL KOYAMA

Warner Hollywood Commissary
WEST HOLLYWOOD, CALIFORNIA

Eric Rosen Architect transforms an industrial storage building on the lot of Warner Hollywood Studios into a comfortable, bustling commissary for studio personnel and visitors. Large, paned, doors and windows keep the space light and bright and refer to its industrial origins. Wood, metal, and concrete materials are lightly finished for utilitarian, yet elegant, appeal. Beautiful, 40-foot (12-meter) bow-string trusses are given added geometry by dramatic soffits, weaving an interplay of what appears to be original to the building, and what is enhanced through new construction. This feeling is extended to the exterior, where a series of rising steel fins slices through the original facade, framing the large windows and doors. A similar form is repeated in the host station upon entering, re-establishing a minimal, but effective, detail plan.

BELOW: The beautiful bow-string trusses bring warmth and character to this employee commissary.

RIGHT: Simple yet stylish seating adds a level of open comfort to the commissary.

OPPOSITE: Influenced by the film *The Shining*, the tall bar is impressive in its play
of transparent, translucent, and mirrored glass.

BELOW: The 1929 former bank building is transformed into the elegant, upscale
Eurochow.

PHOTOGRAPHY: TOM BONNER

Eurochow LOS ANGELES, CALIFORNIA

Building on his success with the eponymous Mr. Chow restaurants in Beverly Hills, London, and New York, restaurateur and designer Michael Chow creates another sophisticated spot that exudes fine design and art. The striking building on a busy corner of Westwood Village in Los Angeles belies traditionalism in keeping with its historical landmark status. Chow works with this to make a sparkling interior that glows from within. The expansive space's drama is heightened by unexpected turns: long, communal dining tables, a stark white obelisk, quilted white walls, a small niche with a stunning blue Yves Klein sculpture, a glass floor exposing the wine cellar. Other enchanting elements include frosted acrylic tabletops lit from below and an arching bridge with a viewing platform.

The tall bar's design resembles the one in the film *The Shining,* and glistens with milky white glass, mirrors, chrome, and a display of delicate glass decanters. A continual play of transparency and translucence is exhibited in the use of glass and acrylic for tabletops, partitions, stairs, and floors. Standing on the see-through glass floor that reveals the wine cellar is a vertiginous experience enhanced by gazing at the seemingly open balcony, which is, however, encased in clear glass as well. The massive space of the building itself is tempered by dining nooks on the mezzanine that run counter to the glass and aluminum main dining area. Framed by exuberant gold curtains and backed by blue walls, wooden tables and chairs are set for those seeking a little more traditionalism within the full, bright, elegance of Eurochow.

BELOW: Quilted slipcovers soften the industrial-look aluminum chairs. The glass floor displays a well-stocked wine cellar.

OPPOSITE: More traditional, cozier dining areas are replete with wooden tables, chairs, and floors, but reflect the bright white of the main dining area in an oversized mirror.

OPPOSITE: Playing off the building's land-mark status, Chow trumps up the mold-ings and columns, and creates a whimsical and dramatic dining balcony.

ABOVE: A long communal dining table is topped with frosted acrylic and reflected by a steel-encased mirror. The Yves Klein sculpture in the niche adds a splash of intense blue.

Out of this world—and into the next—is the guiding force behind these fun, quirky places where the past and future collide in optimistic design. Bright colors, hard edges, and slick materials are *de rigueur* for young-at-heart gathering places such as Bowlmor Lanes. Suburban backyard pool parties are reinterpreted at Backflip and the 1950s drive-through comes to three-dimensional life at In-N-Out Burger. Heading for

JETSONIA

the utopian heavens is Cafeteria; combining comfort with an on-the-edge-of-time vibe is ARO.Space. Nature is heeded in the more down-to-earth space of Nicola. Going too far is always a mistake to be feared, but talented designers create a perfect balance of new and old motifs, materials, and settings to bring life to a lucky star.

OPPOSITE: Sparkling blue covers each surface in tile, paint, vinyl, and metal.

BELOW: From the exterior, shades of pool-side aqua are illuminated.

FOLLOWING SPREAD: Retro-chic hits all the mid-Century-Modern highlights:
Danish modern table, motel-inspired chandelier, and shag rug.

PHOTOGRAPHY: CESAR RUBIO

Backflip SAN FRANCISCO, CALIFORNIA

Take a running Backflip off the diving board, and you'll understand this aquatic-themed utopia by Fun Display.
The hypnotic space is replete with pool, surfing, water, and backyard references of the 1950s—from a decid-
edly '90s point of view. The dining room's pool-side feeling is achieved with classic patio furniture in aqua,
cobalt, and chartreuse. Casual areas are separated by metal mesh curtains. Over-the-top combinations of fabrics, such as sparkling lamé, squishy chenille, slick vinyl, metallic leather, mesh netting, and *faux* fur add cheeky
decadence. Curved frosted glass screens, mirrors, steel, and fiberglass add a harder edge. Five spouting fountains help create what the designers call "a Miami-esque uber-lounge." As if underwater, the bar area is entire-
ly bathed in deep, sparkling cobalt—from the walls and floors to the leather furniture and pervasive blue light.
Combining cocktail culture with pool-side living, Backflip also offers seating in "more traditional" areas of private cabanas or fountain-side tables.

OPPOSITE: Fountains add a kitschy touch to spirit display.

RIGHT: Fluffy poufs recall '70s shag-rug decor.

Cafeteria NEW YORK, NEW YORK

Don't let the name fool you, Cafeteria is anything but a lowly tray-toting eatery. In the hands of Studio Gaia, this Chelsea restaurant is a favorite haunt of locals and celebrities. The space comprises contemporary café, bar, and underground lounge, far vaster space than one would think exists through the glazed garage doors opening on to Seventh Avenue. Square panes of the garage doors are echoed throughout the café area in padded wall tiles and banquette upholstery punctuated with square windows and mirrors. Bright white banquettes and futuristic chairs are stark against dark brown wooden tables with zinc inserts. Behind the banquette wall, the bar glows with terrazzo bar front, matching the floor, and rattan woven barstools for a more natural look. An azure glow directs patrons to the downstairs lounge where decorative motifs from above are slightly exaggerated. Most notably, large, pillow-like poufs are used for seating across from the ceiling-reaching banquettes. The balls are almost reminiscent of oversize cutouts from the space-age chairs on the upper floor—or simply hard-boiled eggs you might get at any cafeteria.

ABOVE: Mirrored insets reflect the lively bar and restaurant.

OPPOSITE: Hard and soft come together with whimsical, egg-shapped seats and steel-based tables.

PHOTOGRAPHY: DAVID M. JOSEPH

OPPOSITE: Padded wall panels, light rimmed mirrors, and table insets echo the square patterns begun at the garage-door facade along Seventh Avenue.

ABOVE LEFT: Big swaths of upholstery contrast with hard-edged geometric cut-out chairs.

ABOVE RIGHT: Glowing blue breaks up the austere, contrasting color palette

OPPOSITE: The architects created an integrated design with visual and intellectual input from the complementary disciplines of graphic and industrial design.

BELOW: The downtown bank tower location contrasts with organic shapes.

PHOTOGRAPHY: FARSHID ASSASSI

Nicola LOS ANGELES, CALIFORNIA

Set within a downtown Los Angeles high-rise bank building, Nicola's complex space includes a six-story-high glass atrium. RoTo Architects looks to nature's complex systems of layering and interdependability to create a verdant oasis in the middle of the city. Applying this principal to architecture results in intermingling of shape and form, color and texture, and light and shade. Seating includes rubbed and worn wooden slats in steep verticality. Lighting elements are designed as taut wafting shapes floating and sculpting the air. True to the design ethic at RoTo, this project is a collaboration of various creative fields, including a graphic designer for colors and material finishes, and an industrial designer for the lighting.

LEFT: Wood arcs grow in a stylized forest of light and shade.

OPPOSITE: Complex patterns of nature inspire the layering of planes and materials.

ARO.Space SEATTLE, WASHINGTON

ARO.Space is true to its jet-set location of Seattle—home to utopian aviation dreams. Foundation Design's client, "known for bringing post-millennium culture to pre-millennium Seattle," continues its mission at the new lounge, restaurant, and concert venue. Minimal modern architecture, with a gloss of futuristic fantasy, is the backdrop for continually changing art and creative displays. Grey and silver—requisite colors of the future—combine with black and scant slices of natural wood in furniture, upholstery, and surface finishes in the lounge and bar areas. The café adds a lighter—almost antiseptic—mood with white tile and laminates, and maple chairs and floors.

ABOVE: Minimal modernism is jazzed up by utopian, space-age color and fabrics.

OPPOSITE: High-tech lighting and fixtures give the bar a space-station look.

PHOTOGRAPHY: DANIEL LANGLEY

OPPOSITE: In contrast to the moody lounge, the café is bright—almost antiseptic—in its use of tile and stainless steel.

ABOVE: Frosted windows and simple pendant lights are scant decoration in the pared-down space.

OPPOSITE: Round tables mirror canopy peek-a-boo cut-outs.

BELOW: Based on the fast-food logo, the building is a veritable billboard
to the brand.

PHOTOGRAPHY: MARK LOHMAN

In-N-Out Burger
LOS ANGELES, CALIFORNIA

The past meets the future at In-N-Out Burger in Los Angeles' Westwood area. The 50-year-old burger chain tapped 50-year-old firm Kanner Architects to re-create its image from a mock-Mission style, to this retro-futuristic wonder. Using the company's bright arrow logo as a starting point, Kanner creates a building as billboard. Fun is the operative word here, with oversized arrows, animated roof lines, peek-a-boo cutouts, and intersecting palm trees. A large, yellow stucco entrance leads inside to the bright red and white interior dominated by supergraphic logo that separates eating areas. The car culture of Southern California informs the design for the fast-food chain that introduced the drive-through window. Streamlined and aerodynamic like the classic cars of the '50s, the building seems to zoom across the Los Angeles night.

RIGHT: A supergraphic logo acts as a space divider for seating areas.

OPPOSITE: California palm trees dance along the counters along white and red backgrounds.

OPPOSITE: The bowlers' lounge includes banquette seating, and a bar along porthole windows overlooking the game lanes.

BELOW: Retro graphics welcome visitors to the elevator lobby.

PHOTOGRAPHY: RETO HALME

Bowlmor Lanes NEW YORK, NEW YORK

Tucked away among the skyscrapers and fancy buildings of Manhattan, Bowlmor Lanes has been serving New York bowlers since 1938. Recognizing its off-beat status, the Office for Global Architecture leapt at the chance to add some sparkle to this popular landmark. The result is a combination of retro-chic and 1990s flair that keeps the site popular with leaguers and occasional visitors alike. The two-story space houses forty-four lanes above a parking garage, so there is little street presence. Making up for this are the expressive elevator lobbies that let you know loud and clear that you are coming for good, old-fashioned fun. Retro graphics are backlit in garish colors, various patterns of metal siding are used along the lobbies for a crazy-quilt effect, and a classical entablature is interpreted through rusted bowling pins. While turning up the volume on color and materials, the architects also respect the bowling alley vernacular of plastic laminates, vinyl fabrics, textured metal, and vinyl floor tiles, paying homage to their simplicity and utility. Acknowledging a burgeoning social scene, the Bowlmor renovation includes expanded lounge, bar, and reception areas; party rooms; a DJ booth; and a memorabilia display. Bright, colorful patterns and graphics were deftly combined for comfort and balance. Although true to blue-collar bowling roots, this space is designed as much for Ralph Lauren as Ralph Kramden.

OPPOSITE: A circular booth rounds out the bowling-ball references in the windows, tables, and ceiling. A frieze of bowling trophy figures adds further whimsy.

RIGHT: The fourth -floor bar is made from reclaimed bowling lane wood and decked out with brightly colored vinyl seating.

Project Notes

FANTASIA

Le Bar Bat
Central, Hong Kong
Tony Chi & Associates. Design Team: Tony Chi; David Singer, AIA. Lighting Design: Arc Light Design. Engineer: Prindi Electric & Machinery Co. General Contractor: Tedd Base & Associates. Graphic Design: Louey/Rubino Design Group. *Faux* Finish Artist: Caroline P.M. Jones.

Potion
New York, New York
Robert D. Henry Architects. Design Team: Robert D. Henry, principal; Christian Schultz, project architect; Chris Kofitsas, design/build associate.

Amnesia
Ontario, Canada
II By IV Design Associates. Design Team: Dan Menchions; Keith Rushbrook; Tony Addesi.

Iridium
New York, New York
Jordan Mozer & Associates.

Red Sea Star
Eilat, Israel
Aqua Creations. Design Team: Ayala Serfaty; Albi Serfaty; Yuval Levi.

GRAPE, GRAIN, LEAF, BEAN

The Tea Box
New York, New York
CR Studio Architects. Design Team: S. Russell Groves; Victoria Rospond, AIA; Ron Milewicz; Demetri Sarantitis; Lea Cloud. Lighting: Kugler/Tillotson Associates. Construction: Takashimaya Design + Construction.

Cha Yu—Alan Chan Tea Room
Tokyo, Japan
Alan Chan Design Company. Design Team: Alan Chan, graphics/interiors; Peter Lo, graphics. Interior: Shirley Chang, Chang Bene Design.

Hayes and Vine Wine Bar
San Francisco, California
John Lum Architecture. Design: John Lum.

Can
London, England
Jump. Design Team: Rene Chavanne, Shaun Fernandes.

Mud Bug OTB
Chicago, Illinois
Aumiller Youngquist. Design Team: David Kasprak, principal-in-charge; Mike Nichols; Leigh Maraviglia; Wendy Neumeister.

Donut King
Atlanta, Georgia
Lorenc/Yoo Design. Design Team: Chung Youl Yoo, principal/design director; Jan Lorenc, principal; Steve McCall, designer; Rory Myers, graphic designer.

GLAMOUR DAYS

A Bar
Santa Fe, New Mexico
Andrew Altchek. Lighting: Gotham Light & Power Company.

Mercury
San Francisco, California
Fun Display. Design Team: Charles Doell; Craige Walters.

Stardust-Sangu
Osaka, Japan
Interspace Time. Design: Stom Ushidate. Architecture: Hiroshi Hara + Atelier. Lighting: Endo Lighting. General Contractor: Tanseisha.

Rendezvous Lounge and Aft Atrium
Celebrity Cruises Mercury
Shelton, Mindel & Associates. Design Team: Lee F. Mindel, partner; Peter L. Shelton, partner; Michael Neal, project architect; Grace Sierra, interiors associate; Jeff Flanigan, architect; Helmut Dippold, architectural designer; Elizabeth Elkner; project administrator; Helen Elkner, office manager; Jeff Bialer, CAD analyst. Lighting: Fisher Marantz Renfro Stone. Builder: Jos. L. Meyer.

The Hotel
Miami Beach, Florida
Todd Oldham. Design Team: Todd Oldham, designer; Josh Geurtsen, design assistant; Les Beilinson, architect of record.

CONTEMPORARY COMFORT

Sinibar
Chicago, Illinois
Insight West. Design Team: Sam A. Cardella; Wayne Williamson.

Veruka
New York, New York
David Schefer Design. Design Team: David Schefer; Rhonda Ebbesen.

Bond Street
New York, New York
Studio Gaia. Design: Ilan Waisbrod.

The Edmond Meany Hotel
Seattle, Washington
NBBJ. Design Team: Rysia Suchecka, principal-in-charge; James Skog, project manager; Amy Baker, interior designer; Jay Halleran, cost estimator; Stephen H. Bettge, codes and hardware.

Nic's
Beverly Hills, California
Unruh Boyer. Design Team: Trish Boyer; Tony Unruh.

ART ATTACK

The Plantation Coffee & Tea Co.
Toronto, Ontario, Canada
Candeloro Designs. Design: Pat Candeloro.

Lot 61
New York, New York
Rafael Viñoly Architects. Design Team: Rafael Viñoly, principal designer; Diana Viñoly, principal designer; James Herr, project manager; Portia Fong, project architect; Maria Rusconi, project architect. Structural Engineer: RABCO Associates. Mechanical Engineer: Stan Slutsky Consulting Engineers. Lighting Designer: Hillmann DiBernardo. Artwork Curator: Yvonne Force. Code Consultant: RH Consultants. Construction Consultant: Libman Wolf Couples.

Bam Wraps
Irvine, California
William Hefner Architect. Design Team: William Hefner, principal; Jason Kerwin, project architect; Sandra Nustad, graphics; Joel Breaux, graphics.

The Red Room
San Francisco, California
Fun Display. Design Team: Charles Doell; Craige Walters.

G. Point Bar
Turin, Italy
Antonio Besso-Marcheis Architetto. Design Team: Antonio Besso-Marcheis, architect; Antonio Cinotto, collaborator.

MINIMAL MOMENTS

Bar 89
New York, New York
Ogawa/Depardon Architects. Design Team: Kathryn Ogawa, principal; Gilles Depardon, principal; Dawn Finley, project designer. Interior Design/Sculpture: Janis Leonard Design. Lighting: Lighting Dynamics. Contractor: Pane Stone Construction.

Delicatessen R&B
Santa Monica, California
Lorcan O'Herlihy Architects. Design Team: Lorcan O'Herlihy, principal-in-charge; Vincent Lee, project architect.

Shinjuku-Heichinrou
Tokyo, Japan
Interspace Time. Design Team: Stom Ushidate, principal-in-charge/design; Robert R. Lowe, executive vice president/architecture; Hiroyuki Kawano, executive vice president/interiors. General Contractor: Tansei-sha.

Warner Hollywood Commissary
West Hollywood, California
Eric Rosen Architect. Design Team: Eric Rosen, principal; Chris Hope; Max Massie; Robert Casserly.

Eurochow
Los Angeles, California
Michael Chow.

JETSONIA

Backflip
San Francisco, California
Fun Display. Design Team: Charles Doell; Craige Walters.

Cafeteria
New York, New York
Studio Gaia. Design: Ilan Waisbrod.

Nicola
Los Angeles, California
RoTo Architects. Design Team: Michael Rotondi, principal; Clark Stevens, principal; Brian Reiff, collaborator; Angela Hilz; Gregory Kight; Jason King; Milana Kosovac; Yusuke Obuchi; Scott Williams. Color, Materials, Graphics: April Greiman. Fabric, Lighting Fixtures: Krohn Design. Wood: Muny Woodwork. Metal: Abbot Art Metal. Contractor: Rotondi Construction.

ARO.Space
Seattle, Washington
Foundation. Design Team: Lanny French, creative director; Jeff Langston, project manager/architect; Todd Minderman, designer.

In-N-Out Burger
Los Angeles, California
Kanner Architects. Design Team: Charles G. Kanner, FAIA, partner-in-charge; Stephen H. Kanner, FAIA, design partner; Keith Coffman, project architect; Michael Wojtkielewicz, project architect; Brant Gordon, project team; Suzana Gussman, project team. Landscape Architect: Environmental Landscape Concepts. Signage: Young Electrical Sign Company.

Bowlmor Lanes
New York, New York
Office for Global Architecture. Design Team: Leslie Neblett; John Herrera; Cathleen Bachman; Gregory Salandy; Johan Reyes.

Directory of Design Professionals

II by IV Design Associates
77 Mowat Avenue, Suite 109
Toronto, Ontario, Canada M6K 3E3
416.531.2224

Aqua Creations
69 Maze Street
Tel Aviv, Israel 65789
00972.3560217

Aumiller Youngquist
111 East Busse Avenue, Suite 603
Mt. Prospect, IL 60056
847.253.3761

Antonio Besso-Marcheis Architetto
Piazza Chioratti
16 - 10086 Rivarolo Canavese
Torino, Italy
0124.26976

Candeloro Designs
160 Cidermill Avenue, Unit 4
Concord, Ontario L4K 4K5 Canada
905.738.8258

Alan Chan Design Company
2/F Shiu Lam Building
23 Luard Road
Wanchai, Hong Kong
852.2527.8228

Tony Chi & Associates
20 West 36th Street, 9th Floor
New York, NY 10018
212.868.8686

Michael Chow
Wildman Group
344 North Camden Drive
Beverly Hills, CA 90210
310.278.9911

CR Studio Architects
584 Broadway, Suite 801
New York, NY 10012
212.925.8285

Foundation
1715 East Olive Way
Seattle, WA 98121
206.860.8800

Fun Display
65A Elmira Street
San Francisco, CA 94124
415.468.3861

William Hefner Architect
5820 Wilshire Boulevard, Suite 601
Los Angeles, CA 90036
323.931.1365

Robert D. Henry Architects
37 East 18th Street, 10th Floor
New York, NY 10003
212.533.4145

Insight West
45-125 Panorama Drive
Palm Desert, CA 92260
760.568.9089

Interspace Time
Dai-ni Orient Building., 5th Floor
5-13-11 Ueno, Taito-ku,
Tokyo 110-0005 Japan
03.3836.7293

Jump
35 Britannia Row
London NI 8QH England
0171.6880080

Kanner Architects
10924 Le Conte Avenue
Los Angeles, CA 90024
310.208.0028

Lorenc/Yoo Design
109 Vickery Street
Roswell, GA 30075
770.645.2828

John Lum Architecture
46 Alpine Terrace, Suite One
San Francisco, CA 94117
415.753.0339

Jordan Mozer & Associates
320 West Ohio Street, 7th Floor
Chicago, IL 60610
312.397.1133

NBBJ
111 South Jackson
Seattle, WA 98104
206.223.5078

Office for Global Architecture
315 West 39th Street, Studio 1602
New York, NY 10018
212.904.1773

Ogawa/Depardon Architects
137 Varick Street, Suite 404
New York, NY 10013
212.627.7390

Lorcan O'Herlihy Architects
5709 Mesmer Avenue
Culver City, CA 90230
310.398.0394

Todd Oldham
120 Wooster Street
New York, NY 10012
212.226.4668

Eric Rosen Architect
11525 Washington Boulevard
Los Angeles, CA 90066
310.313.3052

RoTo Architects
600 Moulton Avenue, Suite 405
Los Angeles, CA 90031
323.226.1112

David Schefer Design
74 Irving Place, Suite 3B
New York, NY 10003
212.420.8345

Shelton, Mindel & Associates
216 West 18th Street, Penthouse
New York, NY 10011
212.243.3939

Studio Gaia
11 Garden Court
Tenafly, NY 07670
201.541.1887

Unruh Boyer
2311 Hyperion Avenue
Los Angeles, CA 90027
323.662.3111

Rafael Viñoly Architects, P.C.
50 Vandam Street
New York, NY 10013
212.924.5060

Directory of Photographers

Farshid Assassi
Assassi Productions
P.O. Box 3651
Santa Barbara, CA 93130
805.682.2158

Tom Bonner
Tom Bonner Photography
1201 Abbot Kinney Boulevard
Venice, CA 90291
310.396.7125

Antoine Bootz
123 West 20th Street, Suite 2B
New York, NY 10011
212.366.9041

Alan Chan
Alan Chan Design Company
2/F Shiu Lam Building
23 Luard Road
Wanchai, Hong Kong
852.2527.8228

Rene Chavanne
Jump
35 Britannia Row
London NI 8QH England
0171.6880080

Jimmy Cohrssen
642 Leonard Street, Suite 2L
Brooklyn, NY 11222
718.349.7259

Todd Eberle
413 West 14th Street, 3rd Floor
New York, NY 10014
212.243.2511

Luigi Gariglio
Via Principe Amedeo 51
10123 Turin, Italy
011.8121830

Andrew Garn
85 East 10th Street
New York, NY 10003
212.353.8434

David Glomb
71340 Estellita Drive
Rancho Mirage, CA 92270
760.340.4455

Reto Halme
239 Banker Street, Suite 4C
Brooklyn, NY 11222
212.592.8989

Douglas Hill
2324 Moreno Drive
Los Angeles, CA 90039
323.660.0681

Lorcan O'Herlihy Architects
5709 Mesmer Avenue
Culver City, CA 90230
310.398.0394

David M. Joseph
David Joseph/Snaps
523 Broadway, Suite 5
New York, NY 10012
212.226.3535

Michael Kleinberg
Michael Kleinberg Photography
236 West 26th Street, Suite 501
New York, NY 10001
212.924.1510

Erich Ansel Koyama
Erich Koyama Photography
1522 Euclid Street, Suite 19
Santa Monica, CA 90404
310.576.0410

Daniel Langley
Daniel Langley Photographer
911 East Pike, Suite 211
Seattle, WA 98122
206.324.7973

Mark Lohman
Mark Lohman Photography
1021 South Fairfax Avenue
Los Angeles, CA 90019
323.933.3359

Tim Long
Long Photography
235 Oak Knoll Road
Barrington, IL 60010
312.718.5118

Peter Margonelli
20 Desbrosses Street
New York, NY 10013
212.941.0380

Norman McGrath
164 West 79th Street
New York, NY 10024
212.799.6422

Michael Moran
Michael Moran Photography
245 Mulberry Street, Suite 14
New York, NY 10014
212.226.2596

Nacasa & Partners
3-5-5 Minami Azabu, Minato-ku
Tokyo 106-0047 Japan
3444.2922

Sharon Risendorph
Sharon Risendorph Photography
761 Clementina Street
San Francisco, CA 94103
415.431.5851

Rion Rizzo
Creative Sources Photography
6095 Lake Forrest Drive, Suite 100
Atlanta, GA 30328
404.843.2141

Cesar Rubio
Cesar Rubio Photography
2565 Third Street, Suite 306
San Francisco, CA 94107
415.550.6369

Albi Serfaty
Aqua Creations
69 Maze Street
Tel Aviv, Israel 65789
00972.3560217

Peter Vitale
Peter Vitale Photography
P.O. Box 10126
Santa Fe, NM 87504
505.988.2558

Paul Warchol
Paul Warchol Photography
224 Centre Street, 5th Floor
New York, NY 10013
212.431.3461

David Whittaker
David Whittaker Photographer
444 Heath Street East
Toronto, Ontario, Canada M4G 1B5
416.429.0245

Acknowledgments

My undying gratitude and respect goes to the talented designers, architects, and photographers whose work and dedication made this book possible. My thanks to Michael Chow for contributing your unique style and flair to the book. Appreciation goes to Mark Selfe for his early design input, as well as to Nora Greer for her gentle care with both book and author. And to Linda Won, my right hand: your value is immeasurable.